NIGHTBLOOM
&
CENOTE

SAINT JULIAN PRESS

POETRY

Praise for *Nightbloom & Cenote*

Nightbloom & Cenote sifts into the dirt beneath the cracks of girlhood, uncovers a retribution of generations, of family and of birth and misfortune of daughters unloved and unprotected, from the ever-unfolding story of patriarchy and its brutality, and sings of survival in the midst of all that violence. Sinuous as vines and gleaming as night-blooms, these poems tangle and snake and take the generational blame, the guilt reserved for us girls who grow into women, and finally break the cycle, finally crack the sidewalks we girls/women have been buried under all these years.

Schwartz, with her lyrical prowess, sings us to safety: "we will run out / this run belongs to us / both out that door with the baby and all her future babies and we will find all your sisters / my mother and hers." These poems are steeped in culture and myth, are lush with the landscape of survival, are the voices of mothers and our mothering forebears who braid our hair and hold us as we weep, who teach us how, once our tears are dry, to fight back.

—Jennifer Givhan, author of *Girl with Death Mask*

In *Nightbloom & Cenote* Leslie Contreras Schwartz traverses a nighttime landscape with eyes purposefully wide open. She descends into "nightcups of hurt and stains"— navigates rugged territory—where most would refuse to tread. In these darkened depths, Schwartz pushes against every uncomfortable edge: personal and generational affronts.

She relents, "there is too much to move, that won't." Yet, she keeps stepping with her gaze focused on what wilts and blooms. In her hometown of Houston, she reflects on both literal and metaphorical landscapes, "where streetlights bust out and stay busted." She's bold in her witnessing though her poems seem to palpate under her exacting "knife, the sharp edge / that we use to make something, / Even if it disappears." In this brilliant volume, Schwartz instructs best in how she navigates loss. "Let me walk unsteadily. / Let me lose and lose / my body in parts while I watch and sing anyway." Her verse though sorrow-tinged—shouts a powerful song of resistance. She bade us sing no matter what we withstand.

—Glenis Redmond, author of *What My Hand Say*

"In (*Nightbloom & Cenote*) the smallest detail opens a kind of world all its own: "I am made of those sweat-filled / sheets of sorrow, / a clothesline of flinching blouses / waiting for that slap and back beat / to dry." I loved this, and I loved also the intensity of being a single person as exhibited in the lyric voice of this work."

—Ilya Kaminsky, author of *Dancing in Odessa*

"The night-blooming jasmine invoked by this book's title reveals its flowers not in daylight but in darkness, and in that same way, this stunning collection by Leslie Contreras Schwartz unfolds what's hidden, whether it's the personal and cultural histories we carry inside us, the hundreds of dollars concealed in a grandmother's curtains, the words we want to say but don't, or 'those wings'—as one poems says—"that flutter / within my cells." At its core, so much of this book tells the unspoken truth of what it means to inhabit a body, with its frailties and beauties and abuses and miracles. The insight of these poems will leave you shaken."

—Nick Lantz, author of *How to Dance as the Roof Caves In*

"One of the miracles of Schwartz's collection is an almost-unearthly, tonal quiet: in the midst of violence, or not, and against the terror of the diurnal is the counter-force of incredulity, the unlikeliness of it all: life, the zygote that becomes you or me, and its corollary, the fledgling that falls dead from its nest ...

There's not a perpetual forgiveness of sins in *Nightbloom &* *Cenote*—there are limits. But just as the title itself is astounding—the rarest of flowers on the one hand and the most despicable doom of young girls on the other—that perpetual balancing act in the book is something Schwartz manages with the utmost deftness and gentleness. One would not expect "gentleness" in such a collection, yet it lies at the heart. An amazing accomplishment."

—Thomas Simmons, author of *NOW*

"*Nightbloom & Cenote* is an absorbing collection that is an elegant and powerful meditation on the author's reverence for the corporeality of the body, on girlhood and parenting, on space and place, and especially the city of Houston, a city that is at times the warrior and at times the tool of war. Every sentence is spellbinding, so read it slowly. Schwartz goes after our hearts."

—Dr. Jamie Wagman, Assistant Professor of Women and Gender Studies at St. Mary's College

NIGHTBLOOM
&
CENOTE

Poems

By

Leslie Contreras Schwartz

SAINT JULIAN PRESS
HOUSTON

Published by
SAINT JULIAN PRESS, Inc.
2053 Cortlandt, Suite 200
Houston, Texas 77008

www.saintjulianpress.com

ISBN-13: 978-0-9986404-6-4
ISBN: 0-9986404-6-8
Library of Congress Control Number: 2018935909

Cover Art: "Ascidian" by Ernst Haekel from *Kunstformen der Natur*
Author Photo: The Shelby Studio

For Michael, for waiting

CONTENTS

II. DOPPELGÄNGERS

III. BY BOAT, BUS, TRAIN, CYBERSPACE, OR BASEBALL

You darkness from which I come,
I love you more than all the fires
that fence out the world,
for the fire makes a circle
for everyone,
so that no one sees you anymore.

But darkness holds it all:
the shape and the flame,
the animal and myself,
how it holds them,
all powers, all sight—

and it is possible: its great strength
is breaking into my body.

I have faith in the night.

—Rainer Maria Rilke, trans. by David Whyte

NIGHTBLOOM
&
CENOTE

CENOTE

cenote, n.

Etymology: Yucatan Spanish, < Maya *conot.*

A natural underground reservoir of water, such as occurs in the limestone of Yucatan.

1902 Amer. Anthropologist 4 **128** Offerings … were cast into … the deep *cenotes,* or natural wells, to appease the gods believed to dwell therein.

The Maya saw cenotes as gateways to the underworld and to their god of rain.

AFTER HER DEATH, WE FIND THOUSANDS OF DOLLARS IN MY GRANDMOTHER'S CURTAINS

After her death, thousands of dollars
   floated out from the curtains,   pouring out
like dusk.
A sky of bills burgeoning into men's faces   floated down

to my mother.   Moths that had stayed
   hidden
in the same coat,   same sleeve. Ten thousand dollars.

Now paper planes sent from a child
to another   child. A secret,

hidden from the nuns   with their   tight
and coiled buns. Money hidden in   closets,

in pillowcases,   crisp with the smell of receipts,
   mothballs, waiting
for my grandmother's death
         to be spent. Twenty dollars from making a
wedding dress in 1952.   Bills forgotten from a social
security check cashed in 1971.

My grandmother's hands held

a belt, deftly,   as if she knew how to beat a horse
so that it was broken, then ride it until it forgot
it was a horse.

Most of the time, in the kitchen   spilling a fistful of
   lard
into a black cast-iron pan.   Watching beans, chicken,
rice, boil and boil. Then calling the men
     to come eat.

At the funeral, my mother clutched
        night-blooming jasmine in her hand. Its leaden
    perfume
that drowns out   stars and the oak trees' clutch
        of soil, heavy blanket   of sickened sweet
    when the night opens full of that expansive
dark and then is usurped by that tiny clutch of white
    petals.

I have made her memory into   wings, I have
shaken them   from my own coat.
Isn't that what we do, take
        what dark things our parents & grandparents held
tenderly, shuck them off.
    Lay our hands in the dirt   to remove
            the smell.

Scentless now, stock-still, her body

half-hidden by the coffin and its décor of   anemic white
lilies, carnations,
larkspurs, gerbera daisies, roses,   patient in its waiting
    to be tossed
            in the waste-heap.

The trick of her body that belied warmth, sweating its
    leftover
tears. Her head allowed   to rest on a cradle of white
    pillows.
And the crucifix wrapped securely around
her wrist, not once,   but three times.

The Gothic Christmas scene in her foyer, animals of every
fang and hoof, giraffes and elephants and pigs, twenty-
three ducks, swarming the baby in animal longing, the

4

white baby Jesus resting in his radiant humanness. *The worms*

are going to eat me, she'd like to say to me as a child, hoping
to force love out of me. And into her heavy breasts I'd tuck
 a smile, *please let it be, to make my mom stop crying*
when we leave your house.

At three, at five, seven, and then
thirty, standing in the hallway

of the hospital as my mom sat with her to be scolded one
last time before she died.
Her body,   the area where her legs belonged
sunken as if dripping
off of the edges of the hospital bed,   her torso and
its stiff

holding up of the sheets, like it didn't want to be touched.

¿Porqué nunca me ves? I am trash to you. You throw me away
just like I found your mom thrown away in a dumpster. You
know I found her in a trash bag.

At ninety years old, her eyes watery   and brimmed with
 bruises
of years she turned away from.
The eyes that hated   the fat or the bony
or the beady-eyed   and the whorish in every
 girl,
tried to   smother them in a bathtub's reflective
             sheen of water.
Then stared   listening to her own chest crackle   open
                 when her own daughter told her
how he pulled her in the closet,   unzipped

his pants. And she does nothing.

That   see her granddaughter   reading a book,
and say it's a way to store men in her closet   to be a
   whore,
learning new ways   to be a whore,

to stash men   like shoes or money.

Letting yarn unravel long and long from her lap.
Ask *how pretty is your Lita.*

Now my mother,   reaches for a bill, another
bill, one for each time   she was orphaned.
First by her teenage birthmother,
then her adoptive father that died young.
Kept by a woman who raised her to be a nun and
caregiver: locked her in a box   of God Hail Marys &
fists & belts and the Devil with his roaming hands.

Dear Mother, every-
       thing can be mourned   even this

these men's faces   laying their eyes on
       laying

their   animal eyes of forest green and moss   on us.
       I want
to spend it   this pile of blank wings   called mourning:
a bird that saves   flight   until it's about to die
          pecks and pecks and pecks that worm
       a hunger a hunger that grows   wild,
       clutching its tiny white petals.

I wish, Mother, that for one minute
your mother had loved you.

Now, let's spend this dough like crazy.

ODE TO ROOTS CRACKING SIDEWALKS

This underworld
Of tangled dark hair,
Limbs, arms, reaching
Up through blackened
Soil to find its way
To its beloved.
This always buried
Body of a woman,
Her black hair knotting
Into black fists
To crack the concrete,
The heavy foundation
Of a brick house.
Oh, that weight
As the family
Walks back and forth
Over her open body.
To crackle through walls,
Through the family's bones,
Sleep, breath,
As they huddle at night
In smothered dreams
That remember her
In the night.
Even the baby
Remembers her
In his crib, his tiny
Sigh breaking open
This cenote in the
Uncurling of his fist.
Give into it, dear
Child, my child.
Silvery
Crack in the wall,

On the ceiling,
The rocking chair snaps,
A small neck or wing
Breaking. Turn
Against the bars
Of your bed,
Those rails held up
To keep you
From falling
Back into
Wakefulness.
All those roads
That have been
Poured over her body,
The years of bayou,
Swamp, all its heavy
Black map, those
Blood lines, bloodied
Mouths, weeping through
The dank womb of the world
Its Mother-tongue,
Mayim of this world,
Always seeking to
Find you again,
You, now my son in foot-pajamas
Dressed of frozen stars.

CENOTE

At 13, the lightness of her limbs as she lets herself
fall bodiless

onto the trampoline, the counter slap
of leap into the air. The open palm of her own
strength, the back-handed

swing of a girl against the ball
of the closed world.

Her childhood
in that effort to perfect the underwater headstand,
legs like a V pointing at the sky as her eyes

blink wide open, taking in that hushed and sacred
bottom.

Now brown girl at a bus stop, all she owns
in a broken-zipper backpack—one t-shirt, a pair of jeans,
two socks, a size A bra and a notebook—her question

hitched on one hip. Lamplight dimmed by the spreading
  oaks'
limbs, as he asks her to go with him. When she says *yes*

yes, he rests his hand on her small shoulder,
his fingers folding over like a cup.
Later, the next man,

and the next, and the next.
Hundreds of men beaten

into one. One by one and her slow
smile, one that hoards

its swimming girl

becoming thousands
of Maya virgins

being flung into
a cenote. Underwater,
consorting with the gods

to desecrate their own village.
Meanwhile, the nightstand
by the mattress,

its discarded picture of a pair
of children with dark night in their hair and eyes,

on a mother's lap. Their twinned joy
as they stare next to

a pile of condoms, needles, and mace,
a man's wallet.

To the bottom
she goes, sea in a little jewelry
box of hell.

ANNABELLE WASHES THE DISHES RECITING A LITANY OF THE BLESSED VIRGIN

I let her in—
the baby howling in her highchair
at this furred thing at the table,

feral and full of anger, claws,
and caves, tangled in hair
and Hail Mary. I let her in, I did,

she'd been standing at the door for days,
looking at me as I washed the dishes,
washed the kitchen floor. Her full

lips at the screen door,
pressing, pressing, a broken Madonna.
I said, come in mi'ja

and thought she had the look
and smell of a whore, who deserved it.
The grass stains on her knees.

The scratches. The teacher who said
I know how you got those. I know.
You Mexicans like your babies young.

      I'd called her back, without knowing it,
as I was planchando his underwear,
his blue uniformed shirts with his large name ROBERT
and was making sure this time his dinner
was ready as soon as he walked in, but not burnt, the pot
of rice   bubbling while the baby played nearby

a piece of paper in her mouth, pushing
a ball back and forth and back
        from that flight to places behind
        factories, this girl, and the parking lots of
abandoned
chain stores, the empty brightly lit mall,
the backseats, the front seats, all those places
you, me and the body we left   *mommas come sit*
        his parents' bed, my child bed, his
and theirs when he took us and said *this is your own fault*
you fucking whore I bought you dinner. Did I have a choice
then but to live—
yes, we had the baby we had it and my mother cried and
sewed every bead by hand on my wedding dress. I died in
that dress, said all those Lord have Mercy on us, Holy
Mother of God, Holy Virgin of Virgins, from within its
lace grave. Lord, Have Mercy on Me. Mother—

Now at the table, this beast-child sits, some
breathing thing I gave birth to and forgot to feed.
She is hungry.

She carries, fifteen, sixteen,
seventeen, the years
and my old face in her hand.

        Zombie child, raised from the dead with a flare
from my tongue swollen with silence. Was it my
    daughter's cry,
its endless deep cavernous sound, that led her here?

I called her back washing the same dish over and over and
over—I call her back—I called her back—

13

All the years I didn't see her in the mirror

because I wouldn't look—the lights pulsing
in the parking lots, the creaks of doors that pushed. Too
  much
to see so I stopped seeing.

This child lays it all on the table,
These haunted tchotchkes. *I brought this back for you—*

They are safe, I say.
You are safe, I say.
You are safe.
You are safe.
You are safe.
You are safe.
You are safe.

Dear Holy Mother
of God, what do I do with this girl
that he left, I can barely read

the notes sent home from my son's kindhearted
teacher, and I need more money for
formula. It's your own damn
fault, puta, I whisper
with my back turned. I feel her hand

on that back, my hand, hers,
I cannot turn around. I cannot.
You are safe. I tell her, my back
turned, the soap froth multiplying
in the sink. We are safe. I am going to get us

out. I tell her—Go to sleep, for a day, a year,

I will hide you, he won't know. I will wait days, weeks
    while
you sleep, I say. I will figure out how to heal

you, feed you sips of water when he rolls
over and starts to snore.   I almost love him
when he leaves me alone after I bring him another beer,
and another, the beers
on top of me.   This time pop all the pills we
can find, and then his sweet silence.
        Then, child, we will go / we will run out / this run
belongs to us / both out that door with the baby and all
her future babies and we will find all your sisters / my
mother and hers / mother daughters sisters aunts / and
yes, the ones I still carry / the ones I've forgotten

INHERITANCE

My body holds pockets full / of other bodies, secreted cells
of my grandparents, /inside my parents, nested / in an
infinity of theirs.   / I am made of those sweat-filled
sheets of sorrow, /a clothesline of flinching blouses /
waiting for that slap and back-beat /

to dry. My mother hiding under the house / of my body,
my body the leather belt / from which she is hiding. / My
organs of wrist that wring / into prayer of tied up and
drowning— /

But also— / the pulp of tomato sap running down /my
mother's neck on the ride back from a farm /face up to
sun, pressed up against cousins / in the back of a pick-up.
/ And across town my father's boy body / running with
all the joy he can muster to every single dirt base / and he
can turn as brown as his body will let him, all the sun's
blessing—

My birthright: my body's water-filled Mouth, / my great-
uncle choking on grass and oil drip /
in Buffalo Bayou as it swallowed up his childhood. / That
endless body of water, always a fitful

of pump and pin, the giving of life / the taking away of /

And the Maya woman, my greater grandmother, / she is
folded here near the heart, that beast / of a muscle made of
slurs and songs: / Contreras, Moreno, / Hernandez,
Aguirre. Cheek-to-jowl with Bantu slave / dropped in a
world of wild, squeezed into a fist.

16

The Spanish of my body / butchers the trees until the
landscape is bald / and yet my body remembers: / both
the black matter trees, those rows of empty and erase /the
    bruise-
shaped branches/ that drip and drip and drip and drip /

But also, the sound of that click in a homerun / the sound
of running feet /
and the fullness of my mom's hunger / satisfied. All this:
/ a long story that spells my name / marked
with a language / to survive.

PAPER DOLL CHAIN

Girls folded in upon girl and
another girl, holding hands of paper

a mask of thick mascara, eye-
liner, owling their eyes

paper dolls for play, holding
hands and repeating

thoughts,
solo boats set afloat

by boys and men, pushed
farther still by the white world.

How to anchor except by holding hands with other
girls, girls to size up and compare,

how their edges crease or fold more than
yours, how you want that too. That rusty anchor

in my best friend, which I held onto,
its breast shape and weighted steady

as she practices her hand-smother and the gentle crush
of me. How else are we to prepare for the Mexican boys

now roaming the hallways, their arms
a hanging hook around some brown girl's neck?

Girls wanting to know
what it takes be a woman, how much to erase.

The rubber tip leaving no mark

left of a girl in a woman set inside the body of a man

or a boy. For now, it's a game of that blow
she knows is coming. I let her teach

it to me, practice and practice the art of being
inside other bodies, hers and then his
and his, all those brown, white,

red bodies.
Never mine.

NO ONE ASKED WHAT HAPPENED (AND I WOULDN'T HAVE HAD THE WORDS)

he smiled in the rearview mirror, he was
driving [

fifteen, nine months old
]

my face [
my back on the hood

she arched on the screen
]

swallowed
no

carried

*felony of the first degree   the Texas code § 22.011 defines
two degrees of the crime sexual assault
        the victim was a person whom the actor was prohibited from
marrying or purporting to marry or with whom the actor was
prohibited from living under the appearance of being married under
Section 25.01*

in   the throat

                                                                    a fine of
$10,000

life in   [prison]
        legs

            held up

back then it was
        her too, homecoming queen,

maybe I loved her [
                    ]there was no name for
        it

cuando ellas abren las piernas

sacred mother of
                run

sacred
left me

stop looking it hurts more when you look

                                here's what you
                                    need to know

                    [

                                I lived I lived I live
                                    too]

THE COMAL AND MY HANDS

I did not know what to feed you,
What one feeds to a daughter.

My hands were empty. I could feel

The space from that emptiness, the uselessness
        Of my hands from no weight.

I pretended I knew how to feed you,
What you needed to eat.

I found water, flour. I made them into little mounds,
Shaped them into circles with a rolling pin.

I cooked them straight on the comal with my bare hands
Like I had been taught to do. Nothing extra. Nothing

Between myself and heat, just water, flour, a rolling pin,

The heat and the comal, your own fingers and feeling.

You held your hands out. You ate. You held onto my
  leg
In some gratitude I could not grasp. How weak and small
The thing I had to give you.

        You were thankful, your hands curling
Around my awkward adult leg. I don't remember leaving
  childhood,
        Like I fell asleep and woke up big and grotesque, a
child's nightmare.

But you want nothing from me except what I can give you. You are full. You ate it all.

I give you another, and another. I am not pretending. This was not pretending. It was the real thing, the thing that you needed, which I gave you, without knowing I could: a flour mound pressed to your tongue, a little cake where I hid myself without knowing I did.

Little lump, little pressed finger to the dough, a burn, and some heat.

EVERYTHING IS ILLEGAL

For Negar Sanchez Tabrizi

The unlikely seed that falls
And takes root for two hundred years,

The world is teeming with people hard-pressed
To die under someone's boot, whole cities even

Of all these walking miracles. The zygote that formed
From the impossible meeting of sperm and egg,

Out of the millions of chances that the dark womb
   squashed.
People, plants, animals, all living things, keep swimming

Past that larger womb, not wanting to starve or wither.
Within us is the urge to live, a whole

Universe, even, of living. We pick one life up

By the feet, from some deep place, and attempt
To replace the one in which the world sets to stifle us,

How everything is set up to snuff our light out
with a short nickel cap. This cap over our heads lets us
   know

This life is illegal. So, call all thriving things illegal:

The magnolia tree, its roots,
That vast network of veins that feeds itself

And others like it in dry soil,
Pushes space through concrete sidewalks

To breathe. Call grackles and their nest
Of hatchlings illegal in their multiplying

Hardiness. Never meant to be.
Every tough, gnarled thing holding

Its own life in a fist of vitality is illegal.
The missed bullet, and the bullet met in the body

That keeps living. We carry both, all those near misses
And full head-on hits. Like that green shoot,

How it defies the laws of Nature
As it crackles through earth, the flood and the heat set out

To smother it. Nature, that selfish bitch,
Wants to return us all to its black hole,

That once pulsing black void.
Who wants that?

Run from it. Carry your light further away
From that break in the universe. Run and keep

Running from being made one thing. In our fleeing,
a flash of brilliance may push the black sky apart

Streaking it with light. This thought
Keeps me living.

FEMININE WEAKNESS

I walk into the school
to pick up my daughter,
a rimmed stain on my shirt.

This morning, the mud-covered
body of a hatchling that fell
from our oak tree,

body flecked
with flies, hard to see
in the cover of dark mud,
only a single wing visible.

Tossed lightly by who-knows-what
and now, sodden, full of something
not it. I don't feel bad
throwing it away in the garbage
bin, its coffin of plastic bags,
nothing there anymore.

The gentle click of its neck
as it cracked. I can't be like that
or something in me will break too.
Sometimes it's important to be mean,
to preserve yourself.

Now the blessed air conditioning,
as I walk into the school,
see women in yoga pants and Lycra shirts
made of fabric that wick away sweat.
Their bodies held tight
by their thin clothes. They walk several feet
ahead of their children, talking on cell phones.

But me, I'm spilling out
into the parking lot,
my daughter throwing a fit
of arms and legs, and I'm holding onto
her while I steer the baby's stroller
with a few fingers, saying
It's okay, It's okay.

The sun stacking rays into
the minivans in the parking lot.
I open the door to ours,
hear the electric slide
of the door like a wish.

I willingly put my child
into a ninety-degree car
and remember how
sorry I am for everything I do,
or cannot do, my resistance
to being weak and its piles
of loneliness—
this whole life a business of loneliness,
stacks of it teetering up to the sky
like an invisible city—

because there's no way to say
to the mother in the restroom
that she looks like God with her
shirt hitched up in a hasty bib, so tired

of it. She looks like she's being
undone, unraveled, just like God
while Eden can't stop growing
in its delicious, oversexed vines.
How can I stop this?

I just don't know

how to bury a dead
bird, a baby, gently

help my oldest daughter
erase what she's taken
so much time to write.

Throw it away, I tell her.
Start over, its better—

She puts her head
on the table and wails.
I was saving it. I want to save it.

I'm an animal to her
as I ball up the paper.
I hate when she cries,
says she can't do something.
It makes me vicious
and scratch-mean and I want
to erase this weakness out of her.
I'm softened only at night
when my younger daughter sleep-talks
in her bed, tells me *wings can be saved with water.*

Cold to life, cold
to life, little children
warming up those lonely
mothers' breasts
and the mothers hang up their phones
and pick up their babies, let their breasts
sigh heavy a little.

Do I want that for people? I think so,

especially when I dig out my daughter's paper
from the trash,

see her terrible letters,
some backward and illegible dark lines,
sprawling effort

in an awful crush, awful dark
crush. What a danger I want
her to avoid.
That paper, the bird,
the women, the people
that might love her
and her body.
That want to be light
and living, even if it
breaks you,
a little each day.

SPACE NEEDLE IN SAN ANTONIO

I cling to him in the elevator,
because I am four and he is my father.
His hat flies away at the observation deck,
and I dig my fingernails into his arms, each nail,
tiny crescent of a moon. Flies away from both of us,
crowning into that broke-open sky,
his beloved baseball hat and our distance from it—
no matter how much I tighten.

TENDER

A child, my mother showed
      me the small closet of herself.
She stood there, child-thin

in a shift-dress. Her blade
      of tenderness, the pain of a blow
that made everything more colored—

her black-winged bangs
      a blur of hands, pink-crush
that could take the wind out

and fill me with broken things.
      This would take me to the winter-night of a school
parking lot, where I was led to the shadow

of a lamplight post, the emptied classroom
      windows darkened
from the want of children, ghost faces

seeking the same tenderness.
      The cold flesh like a living thing,
a child's body folded inside that living thing

and my tender knees,
      the gravel that pierces them
to remind them how easy they cut,

the other working in his cutting
      as if he sought to be buried
beneath my 15 years, the careful carving.

This is the kindness I have carried
      inside like a birdhouse and its flurry

of wings, not even separate beatings

of hundreds of birds,
        but a single thunderous pulse
that has found me, now,

holding my newborn daughter
        in faintly lit dawn, her hair
like singed down between my fingers.

What can I
        find
here?

Draw tenderness out of a cracked
        well, imagine the stillness of water
in its silvery and solid room.

Yes, once my father brushed my hair
        until the curls separated and frizzed,
its tangled rise beneath his dark hands,

comfort in the browned veins
        when he held me against his ribs
as wind cleaned the city around us.

When he came home at dusk, I'd wait for the night
        when he'd turn the pages to my book,
careful that I could see every page.

I rock her in my arms,
        hum a tune with no melody,
my throat warming up

to match her small cry, a turn
        for a turn, enough to last

the hour I rock her, its gentle tick and hurt.

ROOTS

Something thawed last night.
Roots changed from open palms
To finger claws insisting
Themselves into the ground
To push, push buds pushing
Through dark layers that had, just yesterday,
been caged in a coffin made of self.
This is the time to let things root and grab
While the world remains open to the idea.
Take me, take me with you, each tendril of root, each branch
That stretches out and doesn't break or snap or mold and
    die,
Take me with you, it all says to the world before the shift,
that eventual shift, when little things die for any stupid
reason.

I stand barefoot in the garden.
Gratefulness is not enough, never
Enough. I want to live, to plant
Seedlings into compost until its green growth,
Its tender shoot that breaks into glory
is unbearable to look at, that little head
that wobbles, ready to bloom or snap.

RUN, FIGHT, HIDE

*Run, Hide, Fight is the name of a City of Houston campaign
funded by U.S. Homeland Security, in which people are taught
methods on how to survive an active shooter event.*

Living is not enough,
this trek across the field pump-full of legs to fight

the dragging foot, or another man, boy,
pulling a girl's body behind a dumpster.

Because this is a roomful of girls that stretches
across the country, through the dark road of the world.

My daughter running across the soccer field, near-joy
in her unbound hair as she runs for the ball

but doesn't fight for it,
lets the boys take that circle of dreams, steal it away.

I want to teach her to fight the urge to wince,
run, hide, not to feel that hand on her neck

when she reaches for it, not feel all those hands
clawing for her life. That hand groping

under a skirt, his baby already growing
under that skirt. A whole country

of his babies. I have
heard how she can sing. Its
scratch and howl,

the one she saves for me.
But here on this field: how can
she be free to sing, feral, ugly,
sweeping doors
open with her own loud sound.
There is a room made

Of that sound,
another country,
made of her sounds, the sounds of all the girls' shouting—

MY MOTHER AS A CHILD SURROUNDED BY
NIGHT-BLOOMING JASMINE

Asleep squatting
under the house,
my head bowed,

to avoid the scrapes
of nails fixed to the beams.
Pecans shelled under

my legs. Mami's favorite flower,
night-blooming jasmine,
stuck to my leg, scentless now,

that orphaned petal,
which my uncle will later
pluck from my leg.

Because my homemade clothes
still orphan me in their worn threads.
This bodysuit of nightmare.

This dream-not-a-
dream, clothes of real
cotton, a dream-world

of tangible yarn and thread.
Who says you need five rivers
to reach the underworld? Who says

that. They have never
met this
place.

DOPPELGÄNGERS

O GREAT TERRIBLE ONE

The Hindus have it right—Shiva—in one hand you create, in the other you destroy. Abraham was not surprised when you asked him to butcher his son. After years of wishing for this son, he knew his son could be taken away at whim. (Thanks be to the Circumcision of God's Love. Amen.) What Sarah knew was that God was hiding in terror of himself, of us. Even before the angel appeared to stop it all, to call on the ram, O Great Terrible One, with your blurry eyes, blinded by tears and fear, you started taking back what you created. You have hated us from the beginning, and any favors are like crumbs to the starving. How else am I to understand the child sacrificed by leukemia, the boy shot down on his way to slide and swing through childhood, while the shooter lives, is exonerated, and still, we are here, digging through dirt with broken finger nails. How do we watch what happens and still live? I wish you'd turn that hand on yourself, the one aimed for destruction, this God. Perhaps you do and that is why sometimes you disappear, blood filling rivers with or without your absence, nevertheless. I'm not sure why you keep coming back to us, begging to be begged. O Great Terrible One, I have stopped looking for you in the pews of synagogues, churches, fields of grass, cliffs. It is in the voices rising in song, praise or mourning, those voices which you created and then attempt to quiet. They continue to sing still. I see you in my neighbor, examining the death of his grass, or my daughter, flinging her body in anger because of laws of nature, because of how little she knows how to do. You keep flinging yourself back to us, us your doppelgängers. Like a child, like a disgruntled landlord. Why don't they do what I want? Why do they still sing?

With your own answers on our tongues, you send us manna, and we believe you, such emptiness in our stomachs that we pretend is bread. But we can taste the tears inside this feed, this bread of sorrow. We understand this, the world ages, another young father, mother dies, cities of mothers, fathers, their children, their grandparents, burn and smolder. We forget you for a while. But you keep begging like the panhandlers on the side of the road, and we believe we created you, that we are responsible. O Great Terrible One, if we are made in your image, how terrified I am. It is hard not to feed you, with those blood-rimmed eyes that only the lonely recognize.

WEEP HOLES IN BODY

My body remembers itself distantly, humming while I pick
out soap, detergent, floor cleaner and scouring sponges. I
do not want to hear stories about my body while I am
shopping to strip my house of dirt, praying for that future
of mint clean and green to seep into me. Then—its blow
made of black and silvery fists, pain appears, in aisle 5. A
story that my body tells me in the highest-pitched sound, a
crushing warble and hiss, hunching me over the shopping
cart saying: Listen to me. No, do not even try to squeeze
out the sound & crush of lungs and muscles and throat, its
crumbling paper wad. You don't want to write this opera,
conduct my scratchy song? Deal with it. I stand mute. I
stand mute. I stand mute.

Every aisle fills with water. I float to pain, rise to its
surface, a blubbery body. I am made into its throne, its
trap door. Terrifying, this surrender to a creature born out
of me. And all I wanted was a simple child with a face,
hands, and four limbs. Instead, monstrous, and beautiful,
hitched to my hip in grand deformity, I am its compulsory
guardian and servant. I'm afraid of its living with the same
intensity as I am afraid of losing my own biological
children. It knows what I am capable of doing in my mind.
I am afraid this pain is tethered to that see-saw of chutes
and black holes hiding in my neurons, its circuitous maze
that leads back to something I always want but can't find.

I clutch to the shopping cart bar, its metal grip: Holy
mother of Medrol-pack steroids albuterol morphine

codeine anti-inflammatory antibiotics methotrexate infusions and all its vials and IV altars. I want to cut out this sickness out of my body and bury its bones, its scattering of calacas rooted in the city of my chest. Give me the knife. I will be the surgeon. I want to look at this Beast—I want to see what it feels like in my quivering palm. Breathe out in a whistle. What small thing commands so much from me and pretends arrogantly that I am not at its mercy. Breathe in and shut my eyes to how it turns me into a sopping dishrag while I am reading to my son, washing my daughter's hair. A prison of Holy Here and Now, this nightmare made of stitched flesh, fur and infant's feet, my terrible lithopedion, please do not make me your mother. Please for this next breath. I do not know how to turn away a child, but I will. Blow out, slowly, relax grip on the cart's bar. Accept now that my body, our bodies, are the weep holes of the Universe to which it pours itself through. Breathe into all of it gushing, the tiny cracks opening foundation, the dry-walled skeleton pulsing with sacred knowledge. Let it pour, let it crack. Feel this dervish of pulling, as I resist its gravity with all the force I can. Pay for the groceries. Pick up the children. Feed them. Comfort them. All the crackling in the background, bringing me to sit by my son's bed at night and we sing, we sing, me, my baby, and that dark surge. It is a holy sound, a broken choir of three.

SOR JUANA CUTS HER OWN HAIR

> *I would cut off four to six inches (of hair), first
> measuring how long it was and then imposing on myself
> the rule that if, when it has grown back, I did not know
> whatever I had proposed to learn while it was growing,
> I would cut it again as a punishment for my stupidity ...
> It did not seem right for my head to be dressed in hair
> when it was so bare of knowledge, which was a more
> desirable adornment.*
>
> *– Sor Juana Ines de la Cruz, trans. by Edith Grossman*

I cut carefully as if I handled a newborn,

strands falling at my feet.
A curtain of hair threads my cold hands.
Hair curls

at my heels, a sign of wanting
and turning away from want, that furred animal desire
shedding summer.
It is good
to be frigid and bald. It is another kind of
flush.
I let my shed hair climb

legs, cover thighs,
weight the body
in its own dark thread.

I have given away everything, poverty
pouring out of me, running over

my cup. I have written
my own privation in blood on the inside

of my skull, the stubble of those words
leading down my spine, a bristle of faith.

God, take me inside that place
I am shaving myself down
to know.
To understand what it's like to sit

like God bereft, shorn of body
of beauty and plenty. So poor,

Dear God, so poor
and lonelyhearted,

Pacing your hair-strewn cage.
Tell me how you do it,
tell me which part
of the body it will take.

ANIMAL LIFE, ARS POETICA

Those black-beat wings. A rustle in my chest, those balled
fists-of-hearts beating like lit bulbs that click on and off,
secret spark.   Too many people move about, waist deep in
swamp stench, the doors of buildings breaking into dark
waters.   No matter to them. Their bodies glide like
liquid, agile, part of this covering up and over.   So,
hide, little warriors of fur, blood-rimmed eyes staining the
night, the quiet blinking, the barely breath. Hide to live
amid these bloated houses, straining to contain all its
things, cosmetics and laced-up shoes and plastic toys that
constantly sing. Because everything sings, constantly, a
radio tune that no one wants to hear but keeps on playing.
Those *can't keep my hands to myselfs*, those *go love yourselves*.

A smothered piano, a cello, a symphony, in the
tight muscle around my lungs, beating into me like my
own bright blood. I cannot live here if I don't save this
hush, this furious sound—then write it down.

FOTOGRAPHIA DE FRIDA KAHLO SIN ADEREZOS, 1946, POR ANTONIO KAHLO

Traducido por Rita Garcia-Prats

Después de la cirugía,
su cuerpo pesado
sobre la silla de madera,
ojos a medio párpado,
la cara tapada
por un velo oscuro
de pelo.

Frida suelta rizos de humo
desde un cigarrillo
en su mano izquierda.

Su cuerpo encogiéndose
entre su pijama negra,
su pelo suelto, no atado
ni por trenzas ni por Diego.

No hay lugar
para nada más
que el Dolor, que lleva
adentro más dolor y los hermanos, esposos,
amantes, hijos del dolor

enrodillados gateando hacia la iglesia
de su cuerpo, un camino largo
con un barrote de hierro atravesado
por la cadera y el útero,
con un trolley sentado
en la columna de la espalda.

Dolores son diferentes personas,
sentados a la orilla de su cama,

pero retorciéndose las manos todavía,
decidiendo que parte del cuerpo
llevarse esta vez, polio se robará
parte de la pierna, el aborto, un dedo
del pie y el feto del cuerpo.
Una mano para infectar,
una pierna gangrenosa para caer

Detrás de ella, adentro de la casa,
hay dahlias, bougainvilleas,
gardenias, que ella pintará *para
que no se mueran*. Y esas flores
esperando para ser una corona,
sostenida por una trenza larga y café,
firmemente atada. Con esa
sostendrá el cielito lindo,
y sus listones contrabandeados.

Doblados en canta, y no llores,
y adornando su corona.

PHOTOGRAPH OF FRIDA KAHLO SIN
ADEREZOS, 1946, BY ANTONIO KAHLO

After surgery, her body weighted against
a wooden chair, eyes mid-blink, her face
curtained by a dark mass of hair, Frida lets
out curls of smoke from the left hand's cigarette.

Her body shrinking back into its black pajamas,
her hair not bound up by braids or
Diego. There is no room
for anything else but Pain, which carries

inside it other pain and those pain's
brothers, sisters, their spouses,
lovers, and children, on their knees
crawling to the church

of her body, its camino
largo. The steelbar
through the hip and uterus of it,
the streetcar sitting

on the column of the spine of it.
Pain is different
people, sitting by the bedside
but wringing its hands just the same,

figuring out what to take of the body
this time, what language
it can speak. Polio to steal a bit of leg,
the abortion, a toe and the body's

fetus. A hand to infect, a leg
to gangrene and fell.
Behind her, inside the house

are dahlias, bougainvilleas,

gardenias, which she will *paint
so they will not die,* those
blooms waiting to be laureled
on the head, held up by its long

brown braid, tightly laced.
In this, she will hold up
cielito lindo, its
smuggled ribbons
of little sky,

folded up
in canta, no llores,
pin them
to her crown.

TWO HEARTS AS A PAIR OF SCISSORS

After the self-portrait "Los Dos Fridas" by Frida Kahlo

Folded in the dog-
eared pages of your heart, fixed
against the fence of your two bodies,
pinned and crushed on those erect bosoms,

the memory of the man you love in your veins.
Hasty, viscous and blood-letting,
you cut him out, try to, like a surgeon drunk
on wine because she has lost all her money.

You are possessed of yourself, holding
the hand of holding the hand of your-
self. Familiar with the necessity of cutting
out whole parts of your body, inch by inch,

that hoarded wealth of pain and winged
sorrow in your cells, those broken
and re-broken bones worn like zippers.
You let yourself bleed into the

virginity of your white dress, to exorcise
the body from yourself. You have done this
before, cut that haughty bitch
of a body out of your pained

mind, crawled from the bed,
clenching your teeth around a paintbrush,
because you needed the crushed blood-red
color of the last tubes of crimson, carmine,
magenta. No one

understands the heart

until they have had to cut it
out, hold it in their hands
and let it pump in
their own powerful fist.

You have done it,
and done once, those who have
are not afraid of doing it
ad infinitum: for this, one's suffering
is outside of time, space, counting, measuring.

AZALEOS

I met myself
on the sidewalk

walking my son in the stroller.
I could not tell

how old I was, too many
lines or not enough,

around the eyes.
Then *azaleos*

bursting in the dry soil
on Mullins Street

impossibly bright,
like something I dearly

wanted but did not even
know existed until

we were face-to-face.
I want to be every

child that passes,
every girl I try

to recognize peddling
on wobbly legs,

plastic bike pedals squeaking.
Was I ever that child, or this

one, her mother swinging

her so high she is flying

away from her, then back,
then away again.

Everything repeating,
the way the cracked sidewalks

open to the root of the oak trees,
unearthing the parched earth.

Whose child are we if we
can't remember the child,

whose mother, whose father.
Many mothers have buried

themselves in these cracks,
hedged between the earth

and cement of marriage and children.
I have never thought of grabbing

my daughter by a fistful of hair.
Locking her outside the house,

the sun punishing her body with heat.
But sometimes I feel that crack

rising, a dryness in my throat.
I am not sure if it is the want

of the girl or my own mother
who needs attention, whose feet

I am stepping in. Because

a mother is not born

loving their child, no angel
appears in her heart, igniting night,

wetting her eyelashes with God.
No sacred seed in her womb

holding in a floodgate of warm tears.
Even the infant gazes

at the ceiling, watching
shadows come and go,

the desert of walls. You are either
the one who catches the child

who falls, or not. There is no
in between place. A child is loved,

or she is not. And Plato,
he did not say that really the people

in the caves were all children,
the shadows, their mothers.

And this is why she must not only untie
them, let them out of the cave,

but carry them on her back into the
window of sunlight.

You can tell which mothers these
are by the curve of her back,

how much weight she let

herself carry. That part

sacred—not the mother,
not even the child—

but the carrying, the attempt
to hold the weight,
faces in full sun

where, outside, azaleas
are pushing through every leaf-bud
no matter which kind of mother passes.

COSMOLOGY

Let her tunnel
through the world
like God, bare-faced,

burrowing through
the heated earth
steamed with suffocations

of pebbles and decay.
Eyes glistening,
wet with tiny failures

reflected, which make whole
mountains that break
and shift under her girl feet.

God, the girl, girl the God,
falling to the same knees
where no one is there to listen.

O, your blessed fall
in your overgrown garden,
wild with imagination in leaflife,

heavy with bodies
that sweat tears and birth
fruit that die quickly.

The more impotent you are,
the more the garden grows.
Until the girl-grown-into-a-woman

inside her pulls your fruit
inside her too, holy deflowering Eve,

folds you away into

her fat delicious flesh.
My girl now squatting
in the grass, God in a sundress,

showing her sister what moves
in the earth, the fruit
solid inside her, orbiting.

Sleep
now, little pin-
prick of light,

thunder clap and lightning
that she now carries, little
nest of celestial bodies.

BY BUS, BOAT, TRAIN, CYBERSPACE OR BASEBALL

HOUSTON TABLEAUX, SEPTEMBER 6, 2017

A woman in a wheelchair
smoking a cigarette
at a bus stop. Black skirt trailing
the wheels.

Two young men, dark skin, brightly colored shirts,
weaving through stopped traffic by foot
at a red light.

A group of brown men rebuilding
a caved-in street, laying concrete,
dredging up mud. Hard hats and
emergency orange vests glistening
in unison.

Rows and rows of bloated mattresses,
splintered wood, torn rugs, chairs,
sofas and crumbled drywall in front of houses.

Apartment complex with mounds
of indistinguishable waste,
splintered and hashed wood or fabric
or something that looks familiar,

Remnants of a side table, a desk,
collapsed and sunken. Chair on top
of the heap, crooked, a blank flag of no color, flood color.

Mounds full and spilling into the streets,
into the lanes, requiring drivers to let

other cars pass, take turns, almost kind.

Sitting and sitting at red lights,
waiting for it to turn. Helicopters, still hovering,
delivering someone and finding someone.

Dollhouses. So many
dollhouses in waste heaps on streets
with names like Ariel, Paisley, Loch Lomond, Indigo.

People in groups, men in pairs, mothers and children,
walking from streets with names like Bissonnet, Chimney
Rock, Fondren
to find those dollhouses, chairs, tables
with only one crooked leg.

Taking with them furniture that bathed
in sewage and bayou water and flesh-eating bacteria water
for weeks.

All the apartments with walls
punched out, or water-busted
dry walls, black-mold-flourishing-walls,

And that baby dressed in a diaper
playing on a bare mattress
housed by those walls.

Complexes with names adorned with
Green, Garden, Village, Colony, Oaks
where streetlights bust out and stay busted,
years after the last storm.

Everyone in the city feels

some type of growling—
But hunger is not a metaphor.

This city and its machineries, its ratchet
wheels and pulleys, that clock face
pulled off by drowning.

It's the hand-to-mouth, that look,
that kind of hunger, the real kind:
a baby on a bare and dirty mattress.

This is our city's bloodline.
Someone to clean the houses,
build the city, feed the city,
pay for the city.
And the gears kept turned
on the tick and groan
of Houston's bare frame,
somebody else's child, mother,
father or family.
Our city washed
clean of everything but that.
Just roll down the window
on any one-mile stretch.
You'll see our citizens.

AS TOLD BY MY FATHER, DAVID F. CONTRERAS, IN RESPONSE TO MY QUESTION OF HOW HE HURT HIS KNEE DURING A GAME AT THE WORLD SERIES

I called Mike up and said, hey I bought tickets to the game, game 5. And the Astros won. After they won the game, I jumped up and down and almost broke my knee. Was on crutches for a week. I don't care. But let me tell you why— I began playing baseball when I was eight years old in 1959. My dad, Carlos, signed up my older brother and me for little league, probably because my mother told him to. I was terrible. I only got to play one game, batted once, and struck out. In those days, little league wasn't required to play every player. My brother Mitchell was a starter. We did okay. Our team won the championship that year. I just sat on the bench and watched.

Then beginning that summer Mitch and I would play baseball out in the fields, the neighbor's backyard, in the streets. There was Joe Pasafuma, and us: we used rubber balls, plastic balls, we'd use regular or plastic bats. We had rules, our own little bases, and said sixty feet over a fence was a homerun. Mitchell always had the most homeruns.

One time my Aunt Tilly saw us and said *Look how dark they are*, to my mom. *They look like black boys.* My mother said You can't go out and play anymore. A couple of days later she said What the hell. Go outside. Who cares.

Aunt Tilly's kids were güeros. My aunts gave us soap for Christmas as gifts. They all said we were dirty and dark. My mom was proud of her Spanish side. I think she took some pride in being fair-skinned. She'd make comments about my dad looking Indian, as if that were bad. Grandpa's family, the Contrerases, was darker but were more assimilated and didn't embrace Mexican culture, but on my mother's side, the Eguias, they were more into their culture, but also emphasized lighter skin, lighter eyes. I had neither.

The second year I played ball, it started in March and ended July. We played all summer. The second year I was good. It was the first time we had full uniforms, made of wool. We had a real baseball field. The coach was Karl Wolf. He was German and was married to a very short Italian woman. I was the pitcher and I improved and made the Pee-Wee All-Star team. I was 9.

At that time, I was at Assumption Catholic School. We were the only Latinos in our grade level and part of the handful in the entire school. Kids were mostly Polish, German and Italian. We were told we were Mexican-American but we did not embrace our culture. We were completely assimilated. My dad wanted us to be.

At that time, I just remembered always being afraid. I didn't have much confidence. The nuns weren't very nice to us. One time I was playing baseball with friends during the summer and when it was lunch time we'd go to this friend's house. Donald Kruzaleski and several of his Anglo friends would go into his house and Mitchell and I would be told to stay in the garage. I didn't know why. I told my mother and she got upset. I didn't realize why until I was 11—they did not allow Mexicans inside their house.

In the fourth grade, when I was nine, a teacher, Ms. Raymond, said to make sure our hands were clean after lunch. She checked a bunch of students. She looked at my hands, she said They're dirty. I went to wash my hands again. I came back and she said They are still dirty. She sent me back, again and again. I told my mother after school and my mom walked about a mile to the school and got in her face. She said Can't you see this is the color of his skin?

When I was about 11 years old, I got better at baseball. I was always scatterbrained. I was good in math, but not at reading. But baseball, baseball I could do.

The day before the season started, I went to see my grandmother, on State Street in Sixth Ward. I went to take a piano lesson with Aunt Della. The next day, the day of our first baseball game of the year, my aunt Dionnes (who lived with Della) called my mother to tell her I had stolen a pen. My mother asked me and I told her No, I didn't do it. She believed my aunt and got a belt and beat me. She told me I couldn't go to the game.

I was so upset. I just loved the game. I wanted to go so bad, it was so important. I put a belt around my neck and tried to hang myself. I don't know how I even knew what I was doing, but I was desperate. We had practiced all summer. My mother suspected when she saw the marks around my neck. She started crying. She hugged me and said You can go. I went to the game and I had the game of my life.

I remember it was three-for-three. And we ended up winning, 11 to 4. The last at bat, I went up the plate, bases loaded, and it was as if I could see myself from 50 feet above, as if I was dreaming. I could see the pitcher, I could see myself at the bat, swinging. I saw myself swinging, hit the ball over the fence, and saw myself—my fat ass jogging around the bases. When I hit the plate, it was as if—SHOOP —I was back. It was a jerky type of feeling, the most incredible thing I ever experienced. We clobbered them and won 11 to 4.

The next year I was 12 and played for Little League North Houston. I was the pitcher. There was one game that I pitched that prevented me from being on the All-Star Team. I had to pitch four good innings, but I lost concentration. I hit some batters, walked a couple, gave up two grand slams. We lost 8 to 0, and I lost a lot of credibility. My coach didn't give up on me. He let me pitch the last game of the season against the same team. He had hope in me.

The Cardinals were tied for first place with the Phillies in our league. I got to pitch the game. I had better luck that time, 11-4. I won the game for our team, the Braves. I got a certificate to a hamburger and malt place on Little York. I had hopes of making the All-Star team. But the first game blackballed me. I didn't get the chance. Harold Kamenski, my best friend at that time, made the team as a back-up. Five of the Cardinals players made the All-Star team. That All-Star team won the division, district, city, regional, state, and went all the way to the Little League World Series. They ended up losing 2-1 in the nine innings against a California team that won the World Series in 1963.

Fifty years later, I would realize I had once competed against the best and won. Back then I thought, "Well, there'll be other days." I didn't realize that that was the only day, one of the most significant days of my life.

One of the All-Star players was a Latino. We thought he was Italian, light haired, blue eyes, but his last name was Corrion: the real name of my grandfather, Narcissio Eguia, before he changed it. I don't know if we were related. One of the guys became an attorney. Several of these guys ended up playing professional ball, minor leaguers. One of them died of alcoholism.

The next year my dad couldn't afford to have pay for us to play. He sent me and my seven siblings to Catholic school when he could. But then he sent us to San Jacinto High School, the first integrated school in Houston in 1965. The first day was a shock. I never went to school with blacks, Asians, other Latinos. More than half the school were minorities.

So I didn't play any sports, didn't fit in. Playing sports when I was in the seventh and eighth, had me fit in more. I was an outcast. I lacked self-confidence. I tried out for the school team, but I had not played for a while and wasn't in good physical condition. I didn't have the ability or drive or passion. I became interested in music instead. I wanted to learn to play the guitar. I took lessons downtown with Mr. Woods with my brother Tommy. We would take the bus to the 1600 block of Main, between Herbert and Walker. We paid $5-10 bucks once a week. My dad got us a guitar one Christmas with an amp. It was 1966. I was 15.

I started playing. I started my first band, World Peace. I met a lot of friends because of music. We played the Beatles, Animals, The BeeGees. I met the Gonzalez brothers. They had an organ and were playing Beatles one time in a garage. They invited me in. They had me play the organ. Asked me to join their group. We played a few gigs. I skipped school. I went all the way up to Nacogdoches, Jackson, Texas. I met Bryan and Clifford Harris, little brother Gary. I taught Gary how to play the organ. Gary was gay and died of AIDS. Clifford became a fireman. Bryan struggled all through his life with drugs, has been sober 10 years. Has a son, 35, plays in band. I get together once a year, with Bryan and his son and jam.

I always loved to go see games. Started in 1959 to see the Houston Buffs. I just found out Dan Rather was the broadcaster. I can recall 1962 when they first formed the Colts, I went to one of the first games with my father, near where the Astrodome is today. I collected cards, Mickey Mantle, Hank Aaron, Willie Mays. In 1965, I went to one of the first games at the Astrodome and saw Mickey Mantle bat. I watched the Astros throughout the years. But they never went really far. But this year, this year was different—

MODERN BLESSING

But how they loved when you stood
in your backyard, the baby

grabbing at your mosquito braceleted ankles,
the grass dry and needled,

and you captured that honeyed smile, sunrays a halo
or a prison around your paling face with no filter

bright burst on the dark-screen of your mind so
you can feel the hashtag of love and Madonna

in how you lean your framed face forward,
your stretched arm hovering with the cell phone

above your palm-up face, only a glimpse
of the vinyl chair covered in black pollen,

ejecting itself at its
edges. That despite this, it is your smile,

cracked on the stretched canvas of your face,
that appears on every hundredth person's feed,

that your semblance of joy feeds and returns
to other people so that their good fingers

dance across keyboards—for you, just for you.
So loved, your selfie, that self, made into pixel

and glow, your smudged mascaraed eyes
giant plates tossed across so many screens.

Your ghost image, containing all the girls built up in you,

touching and touching those silken screens

against fingers that swipe and swipe,
bat wings across your face, then the letting it go.

BEFORE, DURING, AND AFTER APPENDECITIS AND HARVEY, (AUGUST-SEPTEMBER 2017)

I watch live videos of
   friends
standing in their homes as
   flood
water rushes in from all
   sides

               of the bin which I emptied
               so my children could float
                  safely
               if it found us, the water

from the hospital room
helicopters all night long
singing by my window,
   unseen

               the day I lose sight for
                a minute,
               the days I cannot walk. My
                  intimate friend pain
               and I nestle my husband

In that space of narrow
   escape—
how many times one can
   miss
one's death, and not feel
   cracks

               while a helicopter chops
                  straight
               to the spine, driving joy

into

half-open eyes with the
   sound of life

and all the broken
light pushing through,
   setting off
a crooked path, from one
   end of the hospital hall

to my daughter asking
who saves a baby in a fire
if her parents cannot

months later, as I lather
and
   wash
her hair as we both wheeze
with pneumonia

the bathtub full of clean
   water,
dark hair slick against
her back, a sacred cape and
   benediction

Tell me when
you're done, momma
Tell me when it's over

BLUE BUCKET

After Sufjan Stevens

In every body sleeps

the wrinkled, over-fleshed body of a baby

in its purse of need. Tiny birdbones rattling

inside its round heart of a body.

It is your job to find this now, ripping

seams with a sharp and careful

knife. The yoga teacher calls it bone-making, hip

opening, blood-flow shifting. Find it, this

body that you've buried. This work

is tourniqueting rooms out, pushing those

calcified rocks aside, that coal swamp, volcanic

ash of years burying your lithosphere. To mine the body,

to find its blue bucket of gold. It may be a myth. It

  probably

is a myth. There is too much to move, that won't, it is part of you now, the buried ache sprouting deformed forest.

Someone says there is starshine, glint of God folded

into your lungs, brightening

up every alveoli in its field of push and pull—

But how to find this, with the thought that you will

find nothing, and then you will surely die.

There is so much effort,

too much, to be simply

in this body.

I look for a little, close my eyes.

Inside I find a child holding

a hand out, bright sun behind her head,

a dark crown of hair. Her hand-me-down shirt falling

off one sun-burnt shoulder. The confused look in her eyes,

saying How did you find me?

She is terrifying. She asks for food.

I have nothing to give her, except

my body.

I CARRY IT FOR MY FAMILY

After e.e. cummings

I carried it, my family   and all their separate
sadnesses   found a galvanized box, sturdy
with lead, I decorated   its inside
        with my mother's cavernous
mother-longing,   my father's constant ache for the
hero he wanted to be, the one held tight   inside his own
father's arms which had killed Germans   and then held
up the head of each of his eight babies   Worry
dolls, placed not under my pillow,   but tucked inside me,
under my ribs, muscles, in my knees.   I swallowed
my teen sister's desperate loves,   her equally
desperate and dangerous splits   shame mixed with
horror   casting out her body for a snare.
        I stole from my older brother the shotgun   drum
beats   in his nightmares, the dark skin that people
saw instead of hearing his words. I carried it,   my
family,   tried to take out the   cold burn   and
the breaks.   If I could put all their sorrow
        into each of my veins,   let it sink
        into some graveyard of mine, and not theirs,
        never theirs—maybe they'd live.
        It is not because I thought I was stronger,
Braver, smarter.   It was because I knew I could carry
it, that I could steal it while they were not looking
        hoping they woke up lighter and without memory,
young again.   Every image, every phrase:
the wagon of children   left in the busy road, the
young mother with her newborn   telling stories that
hung amid the loneliness of embalming fluid

from the funeral parlor next door,   my father
watching the   numbers fall and fall and fall,
          the teenage girl's body made to feel smaller and
smaller. I watched my family and absorbed
          every joke that felt like a wail, every sarcastic
phrase, every snap back and argument   the screaming
fights   and I fought them, throwing irons
          pounding fists and ripping   shirts   saying
I hate you I hate this family I can't wait to leave
          because I was trying to keep it   away
from them.   I let it sink and simmer, as if I'd
carried a landmine away   hidden it in my
bedroom   and I slammed the door
          not to keep them out,   but to say *I carry*
enough for   *all of us*

          Imagine my surprise when my baby brother
showed up   at my doorstep, a haunted look
the kind that compounded loss   for an entire
family of six,   plus each set of grandparents, distant
cousins, all dozen aunts   and uncles.   He'd
found   my stash of grief

          swallowed it whole   himself.
          He was born   knowing
how to do this,   craftier than   me,   and
this was my mistake   my worst
          how I let it happen   all those people on
his small   shoulders

and how I never   saw what he'd carried for me
          put on his back   trying to give me
          an out.

IT'S LIKE A GREEN LIGHT IN A LEFT-HAND TURN WITH NO ARROW TO PROTECT YOU

You wait and wait. You can go but there are so many cars, one after another, and you don't want to risk it. You wait for a break, where you can slip on through, go. There have been times when someone was kind in the past, even slowed down to let you pass, waved to you from their car, a little Go-Ahead. You are aware that you have a car, with a stoplight and a furnished sign, while there are people on foot and on bikes, and you are not sure if the places they come from have the benefits of signs, stoplights, working cars, bikes, buses. So you wait your turn. It's possible you will wait until you've lost your chance this round, that the moment you didn't trust yourself to go quick enough, to get there safely, has now vanished. You feel the pulse of home and the hungry mouths, crumbled clothes suffering in their own dirtiness, someone needing money to keep the lights bright, the water pouring into sinks, running in bathtubs. You could wait until you realize it's not going to happen, not this way, so you back up, reverse, find some other way to get to where you're going. Or maybe you just wait until it's all clear, another round, and another, like a patient Buddha who feels no urgency. You're going to arrive to where you're going, somehow, body in tow, your hands on the wheel, a foot to glide you up to that place, or not, Buddha says. Mother Teresa says You are blessed beyond all belief, what luck, that you got here, and how you did it does not matter, even the place doesn't matter, but that you can go about your business with a pump turning your body, the clockwork of your breath, and you are going, going. What a thing to be, this holy machine, Rambam says. "Know that this Universe, in its entirety, is nothing else but one individual being," dear Rambam says.

When you move, so does it all: the cars, the people, the pedestrians, the bus stop waiters. And when you sit, the Universe sits, waits too, up on her haunches, cackles, or winks. And when you accelerate—let yourself go—like the Universe, you glide, move.

BUCKET

At the swimming pool
a bucket hovers over the heads
of my family, filling with water
that will pour onto their willing
heads. Washed in joy,
or sorrow, this life,
however we chose to
take it, our bodies thirsty
for this rapid chute of the world
that enters us through force.
And why not hold our faces up,
why not, take it like my daughter
now, crying into the fractured rays
of sunlight as they are once again,
broken, by a deluge of blessedness,
that chilled slap of wet easing the sunburned
skin and the knowledge that
my children will leave this world
with the wake of it still splashing
in their bodies. Night-oceans, night-lakes,
those rocking boats within us without oars,
the sky folding its face over the moon,
that familiar smother.

LATE NIGHT

It's not for sun's slow drown-out
of the world, that melted blanket of too much,
its smoke-like smother and turning up of the world
its peaks uncovered, everything lit.

It's not this
that I am staying up for. It's too bright
to see things clearly under that eyeing star.
Like a narcissist, the sun only sees itself
in the world reflected.

It is for night's bloom I wait, how it drips
liquid and heavy from lamps,

thick shadow and long-armed branches
all of it reaching to reveal
the underside, underwater, cenotes.

Nocturnal pools
held still in leaves,

nightcups of hurt and stain
that I need to look at, want to,
how it glistens in me. What flaws,
what missteps have I made and kept

in its thimble-sized dark lake.
Here I will drink in that night,
feel its fluttering moth wings
flapping inside me.

And in the morning, how I am lifted,
like a child whose mother has finally come home,
laid her suitcase on the tile floor. I hear life's

click, that sound of its homecoming,
after a night of watching it melt and warp.

HEADLONG

On the photograph "Pleasure and Terrors of Levitation," by
Aaron Siskind

Headlong, body-long
spun into air—
a white man containing a woman
containing her crippled
walk, her brown body,
in his limbs, that whip-shaped
hair. He carries
her freedom in his levity,
that will to never fall to earth,
to be held buoyant by nothing
but air and belief in his own brilliance.
To be that light,
and still be weighted
by the body's core of muscles,
bone and tissues, toughing its way
through sinew and blood to move
and be seen, to be allowed to be
a body that moves through the world
at will, that flock of black birds
crashing through the sky
of white starlight. Not
this life of boxes within boxes
within boxes—

Let me be that. Let all women
and girls, men and boys,
be that, stretching their bodies
along the sun-track to God,
not caring how many times
we fall apart and break,
that fall-apart dance familiar

to us all. All those beautiful broken
spines lined up to make a ladder
to find what is missing.

COME AND TAKE IT

From a slogan on a flag that started the Texas Revolution

Come and take it,
this suit of a body
its machine and wheels of
pain and knotted joy, running
down this runway of break
and sores and cysts and
infections and hurt
and hurt. Suit
of twists and branches jutting
into treebody, treehair, tree-
hands of bark and moss, always
planted and reaching its scratchy
limbs away from itself, this body-not-
body. Try it on, put it in
your death-grip, this coming-and-going-away
suit,

       its white flag of hair
       that hangs and hangs.

I am not afraid of you
on my doorstep,
rubbing against my front door
like a stray cat, pretending
you are Elijah. I'm leaving
my door open because I know
you will not pass over, no
blood on the doorpost will
send you away. You came
because you smelled
me.

Fear
is melting into
milk that I feed you
and you lap me up with a greedy
insatiated tongue, the kind
of hunger I know that laps
and laps. I have fed
myself to others before,

laid out like plate of feast. I will do it
again. Come,
take this broken wrist healed back
into stiff, motion-restrained bone, these swollen knees,
see how this tastes to you,
this hunger for what's torn. It looks
the same, no matter
what plate on which
its served: naked, its cornucopia
of flesh-plump fruit, that ripened peach bursting
out of its skin, that bright hurt.
Isn't that what you came for, Death,
to taste my life with a longing
that never stops.

A LITANY, A SONG, JANUARY 2017

Outside
The birds sound
Like muffled cries

How many times
Can things be taken?

In the same breath
With viva la vida, viva
El cuerpo.

This body of song
Of cry and let-down joy,

To be able to cry,
Sent-down song
Upon feathers
And throats.

Viva la vida.
Its crown heavy
Upon our small heads.

L'chaim la vida
Ya hayati habibi

These small freedoms:
Zum leben das zeitliche

Das zeitliche segnen.

To depart gracefully
From the branch,
This full-throttle song

Caught
In our throats

Gàosù women
Cho chúng tôi biết

Adonai La Virgen Allah

Hold this song in
the genizah of your godheart
the one made of people.

Wakinyan tanka, make us
Lightening, thunder, water
To sustain us
Until we are spent.

A BODY MADE OF PEOPLE

For Nikki Morgan, educator and friend, 1977-2018

My body is both real,
And unreal, made of heavy weight

And wings. To be damned
With it all, what it can

And can't. I'm not one
To repair things, to sit

And wait. Let me taste,
Swallow, be done with it

Juice running down my
Chin. Let me eat loaves and loaves

Of warm challah, drink cups
Of wine.

Let me decide this
Looking out the kitchen

Window. That this life
Is mine and will be torn, ragged

And I will be the one
Who uproots or lets grow

Wild with weed and its tangle.
Let me be loose and lost.

Let me laugh wildly, loudly,
Holding hands with the children.

Let me sing. Let me sing.
Let me daven. Let me pray.

Let me walk unsteadily.
Let me lose my ability to walk.

Let me lose and lose
my body in parts, while I watch
And sing anyway.

Let me grab for everything
With my eyes, saying Dayenu!

This has been enough,
This has been plenty: that in my life

People have known me, and I them,
And I used every drop of weeping, of song,

Of prayer, of care, of fight, of struggle. I used
What I was given, I used it to the core of my

Giant wheel, I scoured this wheel with people,
My love for them, my frustration, my wants for them

And I leave with no regrets.

Let me leave an echo,
Let me leave an echo,
A song that never stops.

HANDS

I made a table
My hands sawed through wood,
My little tree of life.
Carved out a shape
That looked like a place
To feast, write, play a board game.

But it is me disappearing, myself embodied
outside of metaphor.
And I am carving, carving
Some piece that keeps
Breaking apart.

Isn't that what we are all
Doing, building up
And shaping, sanding down
All the rough parts? It's not so
Bad. The work
Is what remains,
The feel of the hand against
Wood shavings, the saw,
The knife, the sharp edge
That we use to make something,
Even if it disappears,
If our hands fail, if the thing
We make looks childish, sloppy.
It's what my hands want
To do which make the action
Holy.

I THINK ABOUT THE LITTLE BIRD AND THE ROCK

Tell me / you haven't wanted to stifle what hovers / dumb before your heart.—Vievee Francis

After the painting, "Belgian, 1898-1967" by Rene Magritte

Those wings that flutter
Within my cells, along my spine,

The tiny prayers
Holding up my legs.

How they float around
From spot to spot.

How should I receive
You today, little bird?

There is no lesson
In this hover, this flight.

All I know is you are not
Me, but some other key, or fist,

In the shape of a rock
Hanging over a precipice

Ready to crush
My skull.

Which one
Am I? The rock

That is ready to blow

A hole into the soft ground

Or the ground that receives it.

Or the hand holding it, aimed, ready, ready—

THE BODY IN PARTS

There are a thousand ways
To hang one's head, to let it
Swing from your neck.

Some girls do it with their thighs
Held tight together when they walk,
Or shoulders hunched, a perpetual flinch
When a hand touches that one spot on the neck.

The joggers and their sprints, some literally
Running away, their limbs
And clenched faces
Striving for some end
That never comes, never comes.

What the body
Knows: the field of parts

Strewn like a bombed-out town,
Or buried beneath mounds
Where something is remembered, distantly.

To be here, in this body! Feel its place, set
Right in this world. To enter its door
And sit. To grieve it as it leaves,
To use it up, to be joyous in its small
Usefulness.

MY DAUGHTER TRIES TO EXPLAIN SOMETHING

Maybe when we die it's something like a blow we send out
to snuff a birthday candle, a blast of wish
from our stomach—and out we float,
my four-year-old daughter says.
A woman's belly takes it in, that breath,
becomes a baby and a woman with a baby.

I'm not sure, I say. Today I was surprised
by the difference the water of the pool made,
its crystal and unnatural blue, clean
and sterile as white sheets
in a hospital bed, how it held up my body,
my legs as if I were able. I swim long weak lines,
making space for the wide swimmer
in the same lane. His strokes drive waves of water
into my mouth as he passes.

Out of the water, my legs don't talk.
I drop my baby son on a cushion of grass,
an inch from concrete.
I drop forks, a knife, I spill water,
I fall, slip, drop, get dressed on the floor.

And, my daughter says, curling up against my chest,
when we die we are just dead
and dead and dead. She thinks it's as hilarious
as a cat in a two-piece swimsuit, a dog dancing
in a tutu to bachata music, the tail
swinging in time, the kind of videos
we watch lit up by a cellphone square

as she goes to sleep. We laugh because it's
ridiculous, absurd, that we could stop
a life in its tracks, a bottom dropping out
below us and disappearing when we are still dancing,
fighting, in medias res. There's so much I'm holding:
how my son slipped on nothing
but his own two feet, and how I nursed
the double-tooth gash on his lip,
blood rushing out, anointing his baby teeth,
and dinner boils on the stove
and the girls, dancing in the living room
like the world is ending, to a song about a girl
who leaves her home on a tiny boat across an ocean
without a viewable end.

And those four seconds of dark
when I can't see, my eyes wide open,
and my husband says in my ear,
You're okay. It's alright
all these truckloads of broken
bones, blood, dark eyes,
limp legs or hands, and across the world
hunger of all kinds, horrible,
wretched loss and hurt stretching into every country and
    continent.

Yes, even that, I will take those—
endless truckloads, even open my door
to see them pull up to my house. Yes, I would:
For a second more.
To see girls dancing like they're fighting off death with a
stick, or little boy, especially mine, jutting to that beat,
hands out, rump out, shaking his
head that it's never going to come.

DEAR MASTER

*Master — open your life wide, and take [in] me in forever, I
will never be tired — I will never be noisy when you want to be
still — I will be [glad as the] your best little girl—*

> — Emily Dickinson, "Master" letter to unknown
> recipient, circa late 1861

Master, custodian of skeleton and muscles, tissues, and
    cells,
Knees, oh knees, and eyes.
You, that distant frame that pumps and flows
    mysteriously,
Mitochondria that nibbles away without a word or a
    glance:
What should I say today
At your little window in your door.

You always want some password,
It is seldom I am right.

You eat so quietly,
Then I blink and am returned to the crust
On your boot, dust, smother.

I want to be able to see
My son tomorrow, to be able
To walk without falling. I want to hold
My children in strong arms. To walk upright.

How do I say this in your language?

I will tell you what you want, feed

Small portions or large, of whatever sustenance
That sends a message to your secretive cells
And those million grated
Entrances, a note that makes it through somehow.

I will be good. I will be good.
I will count, and track, and measure,
I will sweat and use iodine and needles and have people
Cut and stitch and scour. I will be cleaned,
I will be clean. I will be like a nun or a whore, both.

I am not sure how much smaller,
Smarter, more cunning I can be. I will be
Washed, I will be anointed, I will be covered
In mud and buried.

Dear Body of my Mothers and Fathers, that stretched
Past their childhood and mine, into the woman I am.
Whatever plate I give you, no matter how highly piled
Comes back to me untouched some days.

I will throw baskets full of myself
Into your dark mouth.

LA PETITE MORT

The little death
Of being held precious
In someone's mouth, hands,
Tongue

Being inhaled, fully
And exhaled back into the world.
Perhaps if everyone had this once,
Even a single time: to be taken in,

Not just considered, but consumed,
To be devoured bit by bit, both ravished
And carefully tasted crumb by crumb,
To be allowed to enter into the universe

Of someone else, mixed into their black matter,
All their holy and elemental composition:
Hydrogen, helium, oxygen, that tastes of honeyed breath

And heat. To be that heat entering their body,
To enter it, and exit. To die a little for being seen.
To feel able to die for being seen, as if it is okay now
To leave this life satisfied, with sticky fingers and a small

Smile on your lips. Perhaps there would be no dictators,
Tyrants, rapists, murderers, self-abusers, mutilators,
People devouring themselves and others. Or perhaps it is
   they
Who try to the hardest to find this: to be held precious, to
   be palmed

But are denied and thus believe in their own ugliness,
Their desire to deliver blows bigger
Than their desire for tender palms on their bodies,

Tender legs, the cradle of a body that wants theirs.

I want death, little ones, for every person,
The kind I have felt, when I have been held close
Not like a child, but a woman, then a person, an animal,
A world of women, people and animals running

Frantically running into the body of another person
Saying remember me, please, don't forget
And they open up, a great terrifying black hole,
And let you come in and disappear.

TIMES I DID'T SAY MUCH

Nurse

The home-health nurse knocks on my door. She is
carrying a briefcase, which I later learn contains the long
needles, the medication, papers, and a tablet.

*What is your level of education? What is your ethnicity? Do you
own this house?* I answer her questions, remove my pants
enough to ready myself for the medicine I need so my
body can keep the baby alive until she is ready to be born.
With my thigh exposed, and an embarrassing amount of
my backside that has gotten accustomed to weeks of lying
flat against a bed, the nurse, efficient like her practical
blonde bob, asks, *Where do you store the used needles?* Oh yes,
I say. Let me get the container. It is it hidden, high up in a
cabinet, where my three-year-old daughter could never see
it, where there is no chance she could see it, touch it, be
aware of it. It takes me a while to reach it, to pull it down,
to bring it back to the nurse, patiently waiting with the
needle raised in the air. She looks at me questioningly, and
I explain.

She looks at me carefully. *We never let children play with
needles, right?* I realize she is waiting for an answer, I
realize that she thinks I might let my child play with
needles, that she feels it is her duty and her honorable
service as a nurse to Latina mothers to teach them about
the danger of needles, children playing with them. I think
of things I could say: Did you read my demographics? Did
you know that I am teaching a university class online from
my bedroom while I'm on bed rest? I have a master's

degree, bitch. Of course, I know that. But she is holding the needles like she might not give it to me. I lie down.

Yes, I say, we should never let our children play with needles. I realize I am wearing a raggedy shirt, faded yoga pants. I remember that in the last year I have been mistaken for a maid or a nanny. I remember the things that have been said to people I know who are maids or nannies, or the things that were not said, like the friend's aunt who worked for a couple in River Oaks who never spoke to her but said *Take it!* while holding out their plates or glasses, and then would let them shatter to the floor if she didn't run quick enough. Which she would then clean up. She was always cleaning, putting up the lady's clothes into closets that were so full of garments that she had difficulty finding any space to put a hanger. She knew not to let children play with needles, and she did not graduate high school, did not own a home and lived paycheck-to-paycheck. Who am I to this lady? And if I am this, what is someone else? What am I to anybody before I speak, or when I do? I am afraid I need to consider this. I am not sure I had considered this. Now is not the time to consider this because I want my baby to live and need the medicine that my doctor said will keep her alive.

I lie down on the couch. I remove my pants. I do not wince or move or cry out as she plunges the needle deep into my thigh muscle. Do not move for ten minutes after I leave, she says. She packs up. She comes back two more times, ten more times, every week until the baby is born: a total of twenty-four weeks, give or take for the times I'm not in the hospital. I am so quiet when she handles me. I feel so quiet.

Stargazing Lilies

He brought me stargazing lilies in crumpled green tissue paper. They were sitting in my bedroom where my mother had proudly displayed them, their sickeningly sweet smell and small layers of yellow pollen already dusting my bookcase. I was pretending to walk normally, careful steps that hid the pain, the bleeding. I closed the bedroom door. I could not throw away the lilies. Everyone would know. He said they were my favorite, with my mouth full and when my mouth wasn't full. *They are your favorite!*, my mother cried when he brought them in. He was dressed in pressed blue jeans and a blue polo, topped off with a heavy whiff of men's cologne, the kind that would take him several weeks sacking groceries to pay for. Polo maybe. I was still wearing clothes from the children's department, size 13, 14, depending on the brand we could afford. My shoes were tight that day, I remember. They were the best I had, besides my athletic shoes, the ones I wore for cheerleading practice and games. I loved those cheerleading shoes. When had I been asked what my favorite flower was? I didn't remember being asked, or even considering what I liked.

Your shoes make your feet look like they are going to fall off your body, he said later. Don't wear those. When my mouth was full or not, they were my favorite. When I could walk into school, hiding the pain between my legs, my back, my throat, and when I couldn't and fell asleep in Spanish class after lunch. They were my favorite, they said. He brought them every week for months.

Twenty years later, after my second daughter was born, my husband walked in with stargazer lilies. I set the baby down, screaming, milk dripping from my breast. I took the flowers and walked outside, threw them in the trash.

I have to tell you something later, I said. *Why did you do that?* he said. I hate them, don't ever give them to me. I put the baby back on my breast. He is used to my strange rules that I can't explain. He sits next to me.

Over our thirteen-year marriage, our seventeen years together, I am able to say some small phrases, as they fall out of my mouth fully formed, in bed, cooking dinner, when the children can't hear. It was that time when I couldn't look in the mirror—that whole year. Remember, I said? As if he had been there. It doesn't make sense when it comes out, little bits of non-sequiturs, small ripped notes left in my mind.

I stop. Some words should be unspeakable. Some words are not meant to have context, to make the listener comfortable; they are knife-filled, edged with violence and smothering. Who wants to remember such things?

I don't even tell him the whole story. One night we are going to sleep, and he says, *I wish I had known you then. I wish you could have told me.* It is his way of saying he knows—not the story, but the way I had been broken and reshaped—and that I am his favorite kind of person. He is mine.

Amir

I am walking well today. The chemo meds are working. When I wake up, I put two legs down the side of the bed, on the floor, and when I stand, both legs and feet work. I don't drop things if I pick them up. My feet don't slide behind me. I walk to my class and teach it, stand before the students and write on the board letters and shapes that are not as blurry and discolored as weeks before.

At my parking spot in the handicapped area, a man dressed in a light blue button down shirt and khakis, his hair carefully groomed and parted, is standing next to my car as if he has been waiting. He drives his daughter every day to the university at eight and waits for her until she is ready to go home at four. His name is Amir, and he is from Pakistan. *My daughter can no longer walk,* he says.

I have not spoken yet. He asks me my name, who I am. *I've seen you before. Are you a student or a teacher?* I tell him today is a good day for my walking, for my ability to walk and I am glad to meet him.

He is talking about Byron, Shelley, English poets once I tell him I teach writing. I want to leave. I feel overwhelmed by his need and my own, combined. Suddenly, he reaches out to hug me. I let him. I fold my arms in a circle around him. Somewhere his daughter uses a walking device to get to class, slowly. She studies political science. She will do that all day and meet him here, in this spot.

Did I tell you we are from Pakistan?

What do you do all day? I ask him. *I wait here for her,* he says. I know my father would do the same. I have seen my father do the same. Wait in the car, wait at home for me with a patient can of beer until three in the morning, four in the morning. What about the library, I say. It's very close. *Yes, I know,* he says.

I was an attorney for the Supreme Court in Pakistan, he says, as I load my car. *Oh how I love Byron, Shelley.* I turn to say goodbye, I am tired.

He reaches out his hand to shake mine, as if we had just met, once again. He reaches for another hug. *I love you, thank you,* he says. I don't know what I've done, what I said. I feel both afraid of his need and mine to get away. He is harmless, I am saying in my head, have said in my head about many men, boys. His need is harmless to me.

That morning I drove to work thinking of the girl who killed herself the morning before: got herself dressed, readied herself for high school, my old high school, then shot herself in the head. She never said a word to anyone about what must have been some deep, greedy darkness that was smothering her. Not a single friend, her mother, a teacher. No one.

This man is not an angel sent to comfort me. This man is a real man, waiting for his daughter in his car the whole day. I am not an angel sent to comfort this man. I am a woman driving home from her job at a university, thinking about a girl who just killed herself, thinking how I could have been that girl. And how I am not.

We are better than angels. We have tongues, such small muscles that can also be our strongest one, our ability to yell or sing or stay extremely silent. Angels save people, pull the knife away, cut the ropes. I don't want angels. I want people to want to live.

How should we speak to each other? I ask the roads, the stop signs, the red lights on the way home. What should I say then? Was there something I should have said, both for myself and him?

I think about how each person holds a bit of God, not some holy figure sitting on a lit throne with a white woodsman beard, but a God made of people, the God that sits and circles inside people: a studious child unable to get through another day, a man sitting in a car waiting for his daughter who can't walk, his daughter going to class using a walker, learning about political science in a country whose government promotes the hatred of Muslims and people with disabilities. I want to talk to that God when I see people but don't have the words.

Oh, God that sits quietly in me, give me the words and silences to see you, to take the hand off my mouth. Let others do the same, however many times it takes to keep living.

MY BODY STOPS HERE

Having a body is like riding a bus with unreliable air
conditioning in the middle of the summer in Houston,
where I need to make two transfers to get to my destination.
Some buses are like hotels, plush seats, icy air that make
you forget the open oven of a city outside, quiet, and
comfortable passengers; you could live there and want
everyone you know to live there too. But my bus is the kind
where everyone is pushed up against each other, pinned,
sweating, waiting desperately to hold a hand out to pull the
string that announces This is My Stop, its tiny bell sound so
that some driver, a stranger who holds all this power of
motion, can open those blessed doors.
Those doors creak open, but I am not ready, not yet, to get
off. It's so uncomfortable, but I am here, sharing a view
with citizens of this city—the moss-heavy oaks along the
bayous, the ramshackle houses with their noses pointed up
next to mansion neighbors, white-knuckled in wealth and
holding their ground on raised foundation. The poor houses
with flowers poking out next to broken shutters like a
person dressed in rags but tucking in her shirt and pulling
up her socks to find some dignity. Streets and streets of
grandma and grandpa houses that can let out their breath
and be at home, kick their feet up and just be, with the elote
sellers, the pupusa trucks, the soul food and the barbeque
joints next to gas stations and quinceañera dressmaker
shops, the braids and weaves places, the barbers, the man
dressed in the uniform of a busser, white shirt, black pants,
riding a child's pink bike. The mama walking her children
across the street with a grocery cart, the older kids hanging
to the sides. The raspa stands, Thai massage parlors,
Vietnamese street signs and rows of Chinese restaurants

and healers and then more rows of sari fabric stores, Halal markets, Indian buffets. There is so much to see, even in this little view from the bus, pressed up against other bodies, their own small views, some, I know, much smaller than mine. Leaving would be a shame, getting off, on my own volition—I'd miss it, this view. There are no more seats, that's true, and everybody's legs feel each pothole, each road ignored for decades, the-full-of-rocks. What use is it to think about another ride. My body sits here, lingers, and looks out.

NOTES

The epigraph to the book comes from Rainer Marie Rilke's poem, "You Darkness," translated by David Whyte in *River Flow: New and Selected Poems*, ©Many Rivers Press, Langley, WA, USA.

"cenote, n." *OED Online*. Oxford University Press, January 2018. Web. 20 February 2018.

Account and description of underground cenotes from "Watery Tombs," by Kristen M. Romney, "Archeology, July/August 2005: Since 1910, hundreds of human remains of young people, ages six to fifteen, male and females, have been found by archeologists at the bottom of cenotes. The Spanish tortured Maya shamans to extract confessions of ritual sacrifices. It is still unclear how common a practice this may have been and when, and archeologists are still exploring their significance in the Maya religion. Romney writes: "we begin our dive, and everywhere I cast my light I see bones. Leg bones, ribs, fully articulated skeletons. I glide down through a narrow crevasse at 100 feet and spot a skull wedged in at the bottom."

The epigraph to "Sor Juana Cuts Her Own Hair" comes from the translation by Edith Goodman in *Sor Juana Ines de la Cruz*, W.W. Norton, NY, 2014.

"I Carry It for My Family" is written after the poem "i carry your heart with me (i carry it in)" by e.e. cummings.

The lines from Vievee Francis in the epigraph to "I Think About the Little Bird and the Rock" are from her poem, in

ACKNOWLEDGEMENTS

Thank you to the following people, whose help and support allowed me to write this book:

Michael Schwartz, for parenting with me and supporting my efforts, in all ways; my parents, David and Amelia Contreras; my parents-in-law and family Lucy and Kenny Schwartz. To my fellow writers for their thoughtful feedback on poems in this collection: Jennifer Ghivan, ire'ne lara silva, and Moises Lara; and my friends Alison Bowling, Michelle McCormick, Naomi Wittlin, and Negar Tabrizi for being themselves, and their love of life. Thank you to Noah Toledo for his careful editing. Thank you also to Writespace Houston and Elizabeth White-Olsen, for providing a space for emerging writers and giving me the opportunity to teach what I love. To Ron Starbuck, whose support and belief in art's power is invaluable, and life-saving.

These poems have appeared in the following journals:

Cutthroat, A Journal of the Arts: "My Body Stops Here"
       (Finalist for 2018 Joy Harjo Poetry Competition)
The Fem: "Sor Juana Cuts Her Hair"
Glass: A Journal of Poetry: "Azaleos"
Hermeneutic Chaos: "A Litany, A Song, May 2017," and
       "Inheritance"
Luna Luna Magazine: "Paper Doll Chain," "Headlong,"
  and "Animal Life"
Rogue Agent: "No One Asked What Happened …,"
       and "Ode to Roots Cracking Sidewalks,"
Rust + Moth: "Feminine Weakness"
Split Lip Magazine: "Photography of Frida Kahlo Sin

Aderezos, 1946, By Antonio Kahlo," and "Come and Take It"

Storyscape Literary Journal: "Cosmology"

Tap Literary Magazine: "After Her Death, We Find Hundreds of Dollars in My Grandmother's Curtains"

Texas Review: "Cenote," and "Time I Didn't Say Much"

The Collagist: "Late Night"

Tinderbox Literary Journal: "Weep Holes in Body," and "Tender"

ABOUT THE AUTHOR

Leslie Contreras Schwartz's first book, *Fuego*, was published by Saint Julian Press in 2016, which Inprint Houston's Rich Levy named one of the best books in 2016 by a Houston author. Her writing has recently appeared in *Catapult*, *The Texas Review*, and *Tinderbox*, has been nominated for a Pushcart Prize and was named a finalist for the 2018 Joy Harjo Poetry Contest for *Cutthroat: A Journal of the Arts*.

Schwartz was selected as a finalist for the 2018 Houston Poet Laureate and was recently a semi-finalist for the 2017 Tupelo Press Dorset Prize, judged by Ilya Kaminsky. Schwartz earned an MFA in poetry from The Program for Writers at Warren Wilson College in 2011 and graduated from Rice University in 2002. She teaches writing in Houston where she lives with her family.

Visit her Amazon author page at: *amazon.com/leslie-contreras-schwartz* and read more of her work at *lesliecschwartz.com*.

CPSIA information can be obtained
at www.ICGtesting.com
Printed in the USA
FFHW020638100219
50461732-55686FF